IMAGES OF ENGLAND

FISHPONDS

IMAGES OF ENGLAND

FISHPONDS

JOHN BARTLETT

TEMPUS

Frontispiece: St Mary the Virgin, Fishponds parish church.

First published 2004

Tempus Publishing Limited
The Mill, Brimscombe Port,
Stroud, Gloucestershire, GL5 2QG
www.tempus-publishing.com

British Library Cataloguing in Publication Data.
A catalogue record for this book is available from the British Library.

ISBN 0 7524 3315 6

Typesetting and origination by Tempus Publishing Limited.
Printed in Great Britain.

Contents

Acknowledgements

In compiling this work I would like to express my thanks to: Vera Farr; Mrs Vincent; Marion and Keith Jefferies; Phyllis Roberts; Dave Stephenson; Bob Clark; Molly Henderson; Mrs Saunders; Pat Hollier; Derek Fisher; Phyllis Blake; Undine Concannon; Dudley Collard; Jason Ovens; Revd Jeremy Bray; Mervyn Harding; Miss S. Tyte, Headmistress of Chester Park Infants School; Ella Beard of Hillfields Library; Jane Bradley of the Local History Studies department at Bristol Central Library; the late John Anderson; my friend and colleague John Penny, whose computer skills have been a valuable asset; and the late, charismatic Leonard Nott whose local history classes at Fishponds, in the 1970s, first awakened our interest in the subject.

Introduction

Today, Fishponds is a north-east suburb of the city of Bristol. Originally it was a hamlet in the parish of Stapleton, in the county of Gloucestershire, lying just within the borders of the Royal Forest of Kingswood. It developed around the colliers' and quarrymen's cottages close by the road that led from Bristol to Sodbury and on to Gloucester, Oxford and London. The earliest known reliable reference to the ponds, after which the district is named, is a map of Kingswood, drawn by John Norden in 1610, where the ponds are shown on either side of the Westerly and Sodbury Way, now Fishponds Road, and called the 'newe pools' in an area that was even then being quite extensively quarried for the local Pennant stone.

The Forest of Kingswood in south Gloucestershire appears originally to have been a royal domain serving the palace of the Saxon Kings at Pucklechurch, where in 940 King Edmund was assassinated. Royal forests belonged to neither county or diocese and were governed by a law of their own, acknowledging no sovereign but the king. At this period the forest covered around eighteen square miles. Following the Charters of Disafforestation in 1228, the forest diminished in status to that of a royal chase, by 1670 the chase had been unofficially and illegally divided up into so-called 'liberties' and appropriated by the lords of the adjacent manors and the principal local landowners, desiring to increase their land holdings.

Sir John Berkeley of Stoke seized some 700 acres of the old forest. The 1672 Chester Master's Map of the Kingswood Chase not only details the liberty holdings and the principal houses, but also indicates the number of cottages on each holding at that time. The Fishponds area, that was then within the parish of Stapleton, contained 142 cottages, the vast majority of whom, would have been squatters, with very few freeholders. Although at the beginning of the eighteenth century the Crown was still making half-hearted attempts to recover the chase, the landowners proved too powerful and influential. However, it was not until 1779 that all common rights were extinguished in that part of the Kingswood Common in the Parish of

Stapleton (in fact, the present day Fishponds), by the Stapleton Enclosure Act that came into force in 1781.

The coming of the railway through Fishponds in 1835 led to the establishment, in 1886, of Stapleton Halt, later re-named Fish Ponds Railway Station. The staple industries in the area at that time were market gardening, stone quarrying, coal mining and the corn, flock, snuff and iron mills along the adjacent river Frome. As Fishponds grew, local industry expanded in the first few years of the 1900s, when a number of established industrial companies moved out of the crowded city to build new factories on greenfield sites around Lodge Causeway. This influx included foundries, engineering works, chocolate manufactory and a pottery and a few years later was augmented by shopfitters, toolmakers, cardboard-box and wax paper manufacturers and printing works. All of whom were to prove major employers of local labour, who in turn, by their sheer numbers, meant many more houses were needed in the near vicinity to accommodate them and their families. The turn of the nineteenth century saw houses being erected along or near the main Fishponds Road, mostly constructed of the local grey Pennant stone. Then Bristol City Council, under the auspices of the National Housing Scheme, embarked on its first council housing estate; 'Homes fit for Heroes'. The first houses were built at Beechen Drive, in the district known as Hillfields Park, in 1919.

Trinity Chapel, Fishponds first Anglican church, was a Chapel of Ease established in 1821, that later became St Mary's, the parish church of Fishponds. In order to meet the spiritual needs of the expanding population more churches were established, first St Thomas the Apostle at Eastville in 1888, then the parish of St Mary was further subdivided and the daughter churches of All Saints, St John's and St Bede's, were erected. The influence of the early itinerant Nonconformist preachers such as George Whitfield and John Wesley, who had come into the old forest area to preach to the rough, ignorant miners and quarrymen, resulted in the erection of chapels at Fishponds for Methodist, Baptist, Congregational, Pentecostal, Salvation Army and Brethren congregations.

John Bartlett
June 2004

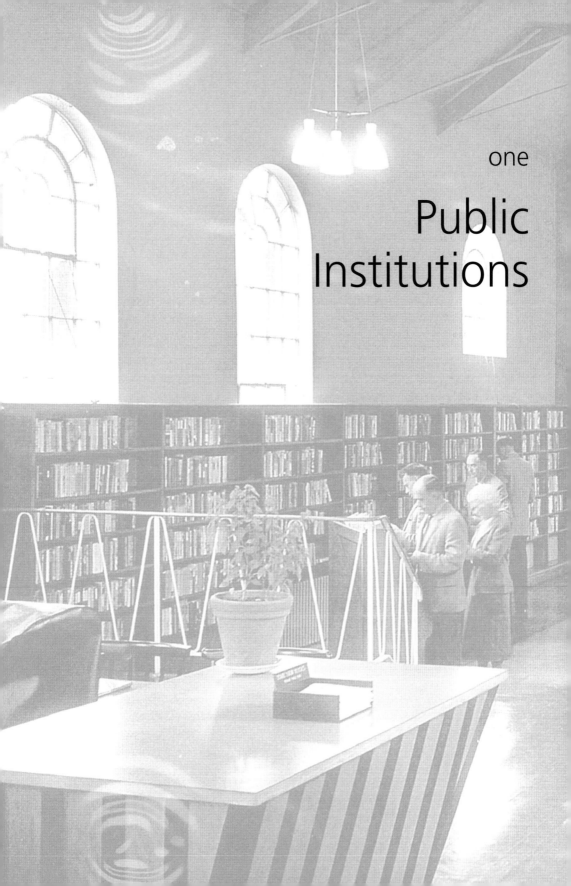

one

Public
Institutions

After twelve years of uneasy peace England was again facing war, for in 1775 her American colonies had revolted against her, demanding their independence. The revolutionaries were aided in their struggle by England's old adversaries – France, Holland and Spain; the English Navy stood alone against four great maritime nations. In order to accommodate the naval prisoners of war that were being landed on Bristol's quayside, in 1779 Stapleton Prison was built for the Admiralty at Fishponds. The prisoners, mainly Dutch and Spanish, were released when George III recognised the American States in 1783. Then just ten years later, France again declared war, this time the hostilities were to last, apart from the short-lived and uneasy Peace of Amiens, until 1814.

In 1832 the empty prison buildings were acquired by the Guardians of the Poor to combat the extreme overcrowding that existed at St Peter's Hospital, Bristol's first workhouse and was intensified when the dreaded cholera once again visited the city. The Guardians improved their new workhouse premises at Fishponds in 1861 by replacing some of the existing buildings. During the First World War the workhouse became Stapleton Institution and when the National Health Service Act was implemented in 1948, the grim grey institution became Stapleton Hospital. It was renamed Manor Park in 1956 and in 1992 the hospital entered yet another phase of its history when it was renamed Blackberry Hill Hospital and merged with Glenside, the former Bristol Lunatic Asylum that had been built next door.

Back in 1855, the pauper lunatics were still being housed at St Peter's Hospital. By 1861 the civic authorities had erected the Bristol Lunatic Asylum at Fishponds. In 1915 the asylum became the Beaufort War Hospital when the patients were moved elsewhere and the premises taken over by the War Office to provide general hospital care for wounded soldiers. The establishment was handed back to the city of Bristol on the 28 February 1919. Two years later the name was changed to the Bristol Mental Hospital, then Glenside in 1959. Finally, after 133 years of service to the city and county of Bristol, the main hospital closed on the 20 August 1994, after most of the patients had been discharged into the community and the buildings now house the faculty of Health and Social Care of the University of the West of England.

The first large building on the Blackberry Hill Hospital site at Fishponds was Stapleton Prison, built for the Admiralty by Nehemiah Bartley (a Bristol Distiller) in 1779, on farmland he owned at Fishponds (in the then parish of Stapleton) at a cost of £3,000. This engraving by J. Malcolm, of the first prison buildings, appeared in the *Gentlemen's Magazine*, May 1814.

During the so-called Napoleonic Wars, the prison was used to detain mainly French POWs and in 1804, when more accommodation was needed, Prison Building 3 was erected. Internally the building was divided into four long dormitories – two up, two down – where the POWs slept in hammocks slung in three tiers with only eighteen inches between them. Today this building is in use as nurses' accommodation.

Above: Still standing next to the hospital (red) entrance is the former guardhouse and mess hall for the militiamen. With the regular army away fighting overseas, the militia and volunteers' regiments had been mobilised in fear of a French invasion. The various regiments of militia, who had been assigned garrison duties in Bristol, were also responsible for guarding the prisoners. Notably among these were the Monmouth militia, who were described as being 'of smart and military appearance'.

Bottom left: A Monmouth militiaman, Grenadier Company.

Bottom right: A Monmouth militiaman, Battalion Company.

Still standing in Manor road, adjacent to the hospital, is the former Officers' Mess House, which was used by the militia officers under the command of Lord Bateman, Colonel of the Herefordshire Militia, who was in charge of security when the prison was in use. To his credit, Col Bateman banned all visitors – he would not let the prisoners be exhibited 'like wild beasts at a fair'.

Also, still standing close to Blackberry Hill Hospital in Manor Road, is the former Admiralty Agent's House, seen here in 1970. Though larger than the Officers' Mess House, both houses can still be recognised as typical Georgian military buildings. The agent was a civilian who ran the prison on behalf of the Admiralty.

The misery of the French POWs came to an end in 1814, with the treaty of Paris. The prisoners left in order of capture; those imprisoned for eleven years or more going first. At the rear of the ex-prison building is a plaque, erected in 1933, by the French Circle of Friends at Bristol to commemorate their compatriots who died and were interred within the prison walls.

A LA MÉMOIRE
DES
SOLDATS FRANÇAIS
INTERNÉS ET ENTERRÉS ICI 1782 - 1820.
LE CERCLE FRANÇAIS DE BRISTOL ET AMIS
1933.

The French Circle of Friends have still not forgotten the POWs who died here at Fishponds and on occasions hold a commemorative service, conducted in French, complete with a priest, in front of their plaque.

The Incorporation of the Poor, having acquired 'the old French prison' in 1832 for use as a workhouse to relieve the extreme overcrowding at St Peter's Hospital (Bristol's first workhouse), had by 1860 demolished some of the old prison buildings and new buildings were added. Here Mr Perry, Governor of the Guardians, lays the foundation stone. Note the internal yard walls separating the buildings.

In this modern view of the old guardhouse and the nurses' home, taken from the same view point as the previous picture, the internal yard walls have been removed, c. 1975.

The Master and Matron of Stapleton Workhouse, holders of the joint married appointment, lived in some comfort in their apartment that projected from the front of the 1861 building facing the lodge; where if a member of staff dared to arrive late for duty they could be seen by matron.

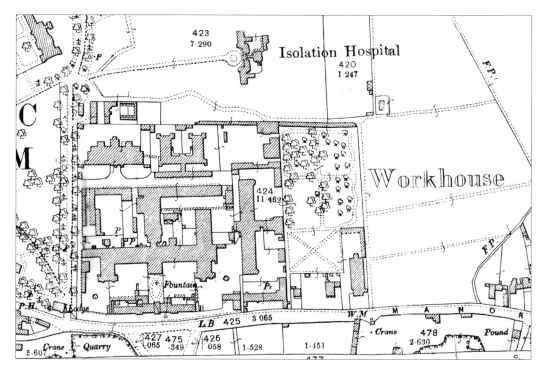

This plan of the workhouse, extracted from the 1908 Ordnance Survey map, shows the extent of the buildings. The tree-planted area, at the north-east corner of the premises within the walls, was the cemetery of the old prison.

On the 27 September 1940 the German Air Force attempted a daylight raid on the Parnall aircraft factory at Yate, near Bristol. A German Messerschmitt 110 was shot down by Flying Officer Michael Royce, flying a British Hurricane. The Messerschmitt crashed into the courtyard of the hospital (then known as Manor Park) killing the two crew members. This was the only enemy aircraft to crash in Bristol during the Second World War.

The bodies of the German airmen were recovered from the crash site and the pilot, twenty-seven year old Oberfeldwebel Hans Tiepelt and his gunner Unteroffizier Herbert Brosig, aged twenty-one, were laid to rest in the military section of nearby Greenbank Cemetery.

St Peter's Hospital was erected as a dwelling in the late twelfth century, refurbished by Robert Aldworth around 1612 before becoming a sugar refinery, and a mint in 1695. It was purchased by the Guardians of the Poor in 1698 and turned into a workhouse for a hundred boys, with a pair of stocks and a whipping post set up in the yard. It was later known as a hospital because they took in sick paupers and idiots. Its last use, within living memory, was for the registering of births, deaths and marriages. It was destroyed by enemy bombers on the 24 November 1940 when Castle Street and the centre of Bristol was devastated. It was perhaps the most serious architectural loss that Bristol suffered in the Blitz. Fishponds has a direct link with St Peter's Hospital, for it was from here that the paupers were transferred in 1832 (see p. 15). Later when the Bristol Lunatic Asylum was built at Fishponds, the pauper lunatics in St Peter's were also sent from the old hospital to modern accommodation at Fishponds.

In 1855 the pauper lunatics were still housed at St Peter's Hospital, but at the insistence of the government, Bristol had to build itself an asylum. This picture depicts the architects' drawing and plan – the projected cost was £40,000.

When the Bristol Lunatic Asylum was opened in 1861, it was the first public hospital to provide accommodation for the mentally ill. Regarded as a model building, authorities came from all over England to view and copy it. Of the first 115 patients received from St Peter's, the commissioners reported, the improvement was such, that 'they could hardly recognise the patients before them as those they had been accustomed to see in St Peter's'.

The asylum was renamed the Bristol Mental Hospital in 1921. Originally designed for 250 patients, the building became overcrowded and several wings were added, increasing its capacity to 800. This aerial picture shows the lodge at the main entrance in the lower right corner and the wall and a row of trees along Manor Road screening the buildings from public view.

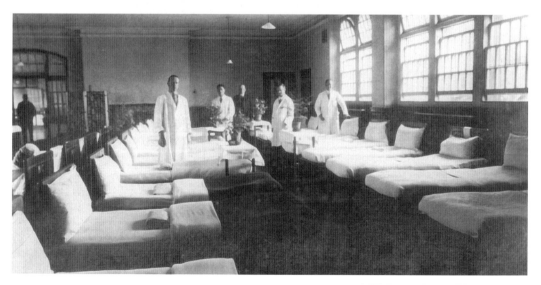

One of the huge ninety-bed wards of the mental hospital, c. 1925. Under the Mental Health Act of 1959 the asylum was renamed Glenside.

Beaufort War Hospital, Fishponds, Bristol. 1478.

During the First World War, with British casualties increasing, the War Office had urgent need for more beds for sick and wounded soldiers so patients at the Bristol Asylum were sent to other asylums, thus freeing the buildings for use as a military hospital. The Duke of Beaufort was asked if his name might be used. He agreed and so the Beaufort War Hospital came into being.

Ward No 16 Beaufort War Hospital. Fishponds, Bristol 1527.

Having survived the journey home from the front, wounded soldiers, some little more than boys, are seen here in Ward 16 at the Beaufort War Hospital.

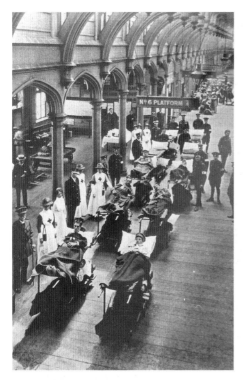

Wounded soldiers on stretchers arriving at Temple Meads Railway Station, Bristol, before being sent on to their allocated hospital. The railway platform is part of the original station, recently known as the Brunel Shed and currently houses the British Empire & Commonwealth Museum.

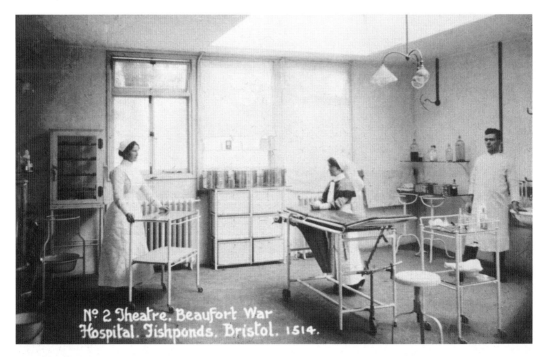

Operating Theatre 2, looking quite primitive by today's standards. Dr J. Blackford who had been Medical Superintendent of the asylum, was appointed Commanding Officer with the rank of Lt Colonel.

The laundry where the bedsheets and washing for the whole hospital was done by the laundry maids. Note the large hand-operated mangle on the raised floor.

The lodge with its tall chimney at the main entrance of the hospital still stands today, though the pillars at the gateway, the lamp, the iron railings and the flagpole have all gone.

Many local churches and ordinary citizens organized concerts and events to entertain the wounded troops. Here in the drive of the hospital, recuperating soldiers gather to be taken on an outing. The work of the hospital ceased on 28 February 1919, by which date the total number of patients received had reached 29,439.

Built in 1847 to house all the indoor poor of the Clifton Poor Law Union, which was renamed the Barton Regis Union in 1877, Eastville Workhouse eventually came under the control of Bristol City Council's Health Committee in 1930. They maintained the establishment from 1948 as a home for the care of the aged, although it was universally known as 'No. 100 Fishponds Road'. It was finally demolished in 1972 to make way for residential housing.

Mr John Edmond Blake, a foreman printer, of No. 43 Lodge Causeway, built Fishponds Picture House at the corner of Station Avenue and Fishponds Road, in 1911. The cinema had several owners before coming into the hands of Sid Macaire. However, unable to compete with the new 1,200 seat Vandyke cinema nearby, Mr Macaire sold out to the Bristol City Council in August 1926 for £2,500.

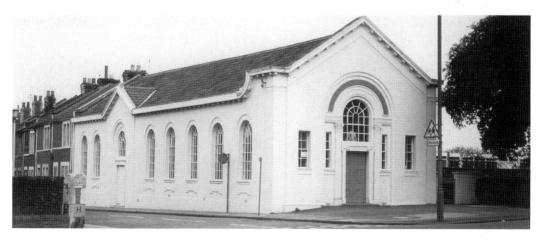

The former Picture House became Fishponds Library, pictured here in 1973 before the houses to its rear were demolished. Opened by the Lord Mayor Councillor J. Curle in December 1927, the new accommodation consisted of three departments: a lending library for adults; a general reading room and a children's department.

Fishponds' first public library had been established in 1900, when a news and reading room at the old Ridgeway Board School, Fishponds Road, had been opened. That arrangement came to an end in 1918, when a classroom at Alexandra Park School was utilised until the libraries committee purchased the former picture hall.

On the left is Mr L. Acland Taylor FLA, city librarian and on the right is Mr W.S. Skinner, architect who was responsible for converting Fishponds Picture House into a public library in 1927.

When Fishponds' library was opened in 1927, the public was admitted through the side entrance in Station Avenue and the desk, where books on loan were date stamped before being released, was situated facing the door.

The Fishponds library of 1927 provided a reading room for the public, by partitioning off the whole end of the building where the present day entrance is situated, facing Fishponds Road.

The library was modernised in 1960 – the side entrance from Station Avenue was closed off and the current floor layout adopted, with the desk moved to the main road end of the building. A separate entry and exit also provided.

The 1960 alterations remain little changed, except for the space through the arches to the right in this picture, which has now become the librarians' office.

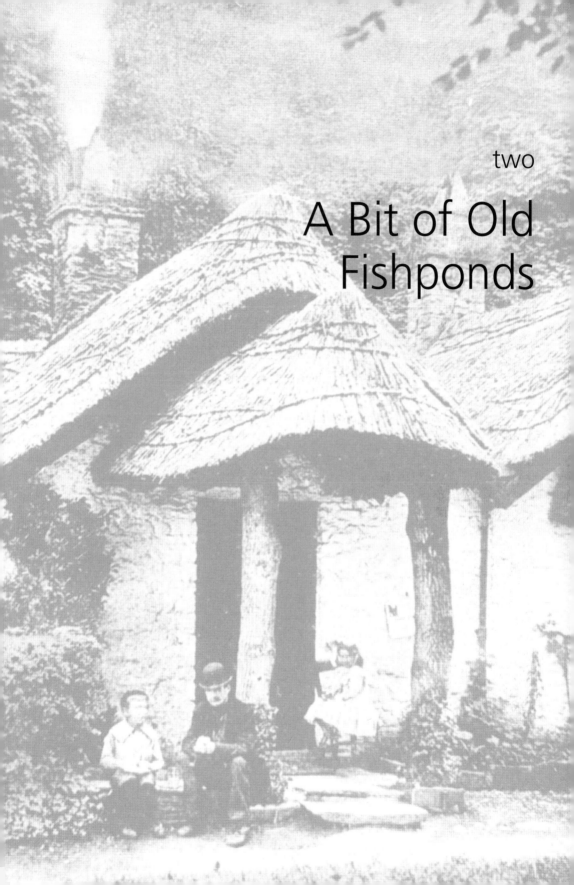

two

A Bit of Old
Fishponds

Built in the early 1700s, Fishponds Charity School is one of the oldest buildings in the locality. It was due to the generosity of one Mary Webb, who in her will dated 15 October 1729 bequeathed to her friends, John Berkeley and several other persons, the sum of £450, that they and their survivors should after her death, invest and from the interest thereof, provide for a master or teacher for the school built by her near the fish ponds in the parish of Stapleton, to educate twenty poor boys and ten poor girls of the parish. Further, that twelve pence per week be paid to three old women of the parish who were to be lodged in the rooms adjoining the schoolhouse. Other well-meaning people added to the capital of the charity and a number of trustees were appointed. The Mary Webb charity survives to this day.

Opposite above and below: These picturesque cottages in Guinea Lane (seen here around 1910) were subject of a demolition order in 1937 and were described as having bulging, perished stonework with settlement cracks, rising and penetrating damp and decayed woodwork. The rooms were poorly lit with small windows and low ceilings. The water supply consisted of an outside tap shared between four cottages and the non-flushing WCs were in a dilapidated compartment 63ft from the back door of No. 4. Rents varied from 3s a week to 6s 6d. Only two cottages close to the church have survived and the rest were demolished and replaced by garages.

Guinea Lane, Fishponds.

Channell House, seen here in 1936 falling into disrepair, was situated in Channell's Hill (now Channon's Hill) and is marked on Chester Master's 1610 map of the Kingswood Forest. It was thought to have been a farmhouse of fifteenth-century origin and close by was a barn and cottages that survived until, *c.* 1968.

These cottages and barn were formerly part of the outbuildings of Channell House, where in 1935, Mr Fredrick Charles Carnell carried on his business as a firewood dealer.

left: One of the Carnell children is seen here playing on the cottage lawn with the ancient barn, that had an outside stone staircase leading to the upper storey, behind her. By the early 1940s Mr Alfred Hutton, transport contractor, was operating from No. 92 Channon's Hill. A Mr Pearce was operating a grocery business from the little shop just before these buildings and the barn were demolished around 1968 to make way for a Great Mills store.

Below: Both pictures depict Mr Hutton's transport business that became Mr Pearce's grocery shop before demolition.

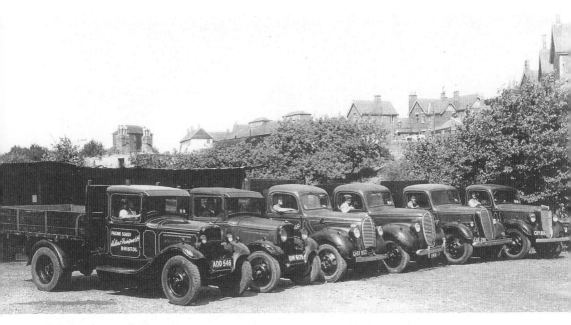

Mr Hutton's fleet of lorries with their drivers pose for the camera at the Channons Hill premises, *c.* 1940. The roofs of the Snowdon Road Children's Home, built in the 1920s, can be seen above the bushes.

The Salvation Army Citadel in Channon's Hill was opened 16 March 1916. It was built of red brick and Bath stone to accommodate 300 persons and the building cost £1,362. The opening ceremony was performed by Mr W.H. Greville Edwards in the absence of his sister the Hon. Mrs Smythe who was seriously indisposed. The Salvation Army remained at Channon's Hill until 1973 and the building is now in commercial use.

Leonard Stamp, haulier, traded from premises in Blackberry Hill from 1950 until 1962 when he moved his business to larger premises at Avonmouth. Seen here with Snowdon Road in the background is Mr Stamp's new tanker lorry, which was a great acquisition to his fleet in 1952.

Just behind this old cottage in Pound Lane, off Manor Road, used to stand the village pound, where stray cattle and livestock were impounded and only released to the owner on payment of a fee.

Despite the Old Tavern pub, at the top of Blackberry Hill, bearing a date of 1877 on its rear façade, Thomas Charles Hutton is recorded as the licensee (and presumably brewer) here in 1869. The brewery malthouse still stands, only slightly altered, but the house at the fork of the road in front of the inn has been demolished and the space now provides a small car park.

Christmas festivities 1953 at the Old Tavern, Blackberry Hill. The licensee, Mrs Shepard, is seated at the centre of the second row from the front.

Local tradition has it that a council of war between General Fairfax and his Commander of Cavalry, Oliver Cromwell, took place at Wickham Court (a sixteenth-century farmhouse, just above Wickham Bridge, Stapleton) to discuss their plan of campaign for the re-taking of Bristol in 1645. The court is seen here in 1975.

Looking down on Wickham Court and its ancillary outbuildings from the east, with the river Frome beyond, in 1975. Today the court and its environs have been converted into six separate homes.

While it's highly probable that Oliver Cromwell was at Stapleton during the English Civil War, it was upon the flimsy evidence of some ancient weapons being found concealed in the roof of the court house in the 1930s, that a plaque to commemorate the council of war was erected on 8 June 1949 by the Cromwell Association, Alderman Sir John Inskip and local historian Fredrick C. Jones.

Wickham Court itself looks down upon the medieval Wickham bridge, seen here, *c.* 1915. It was the only substantial stone bridge in the immediate neighbourhood, during the English Civil War, capable of allowing an army with its guns and baggage trains to cross the river Frome dryshod.

Oldbury Court House has had many owners during its long history. The names of some are perpetuated in the street names of the district – Dodisham, Delabere and Graeme. But none is better known than that of the Vassall family, whose association with the house and estate was to last for over a hundred years.

After Thomas Graeme acquired Oldbury Court in 1799 he engaged Humphrey Repton, the landscape gardener, to remodel the estate. Among Repton's substantial changes to the parkland, was the addition of this quaint, thatched rustic cottage at the Frenchay entrance to the estate.

Above: Although William Vassall, an army doctor, inherited a share of Oldbury Court, he made no claim upon the estate in lieu of debts incurred by his late father Henry Vassall. The doctor's younger son, Robert Lowe Grant Vassall, purchased Oldbury Court in 1871. His fourth son Harry Graeme Vassall (seen here) sold the estate to Bristol City Council in 1937, who turned its 115 acres into a public park.

Right: Mr and Mrs Bawn pictured posing for the camera, *c.* 1896. Mrs Bawn was employed as the cook at Oldbury Court House.

The entry to Oldbury Court from Fishponds, via Oldbury Court Road, is known locally as 'the White Gate'. Here a lady visitor pauses to pass the time of day with the ranger, *c.* 1910.

Mr James Williams, proprietor of Fishponds Steam Laundry (1877-1946) pictured in the garden of his house, with his family and dog, *c.* 1900. The laundry building stood immediately alongside the house.

Mr Williams' fleet of delivery vans parked in the field at the rear of the laundry, *c.* 1920. The field, where in the early days washing was hung out to dry, is known to this day as 'the laundry field'.

In the 1920s it was possible to buy just a chassis fitted with an engine, the owner could then have a body of choice fitted. Note the chain drive to the rear wheels that are fitted with solid rubber tyres and the exposed cart-like suspension springs fitted to the front axle on Mr Williams' delivery van.

Dr Joseph Mason came from Wickwar, Gloucestershire, in 1741 and established a private lunatic asylum at Fishponds in the premises that later became Fishponds Laundry. Unfortunately those same buildings were destroyed by fire in 1972, when in the possession of the Hygienic Straw Co. and the ancient house was demolished to make way for a housing development known as College Court.

Dr Mason prospered at Fishponds and, around 1760, built Fishponds House, an imposing four-storey mansion, on a site between College Road and Oldbury Court Road, straddling what is now Victoria Park. The doctor removed his asylum to his new house that contained around twenty-five bedrooms for family, staff and patients and an unusual feature for its day, – a private chapel.

When Fishponds House came up
for sale in 1859 it was purchased by
Henry Collyer Massingham, the well-
known boot manufacturer, who had
opened his first boot factory in Old
Market, Bristol. At this time the house
contained around ninety-nine rooms;
the central portion was used as the
private residence, while the wings,
outside portions and the rear were
used as the boot manufactory.

This stylised painting of Massingham's boot manufactory, used for advertising purposes, shows its
location near St Mary's church, on what became Manor Road. In 1869 Mr Massingham moved on
and the house became a school until about 1879. Then, in the early 1880s, Fishponds House was
demolished and the site and grounds laid out for building.

John Yalland came from Devon to Bristol, to found a building and contracting business. He became resident at Fishponds around 1854, where he purchased land and developed a twelve-acre residential estate, converting an old farmhouse into a grand residence that he called The Manor House, shown here in this rare picture from the late 1920s. The house and estate was sold in 1936, subsequently the house was demolished and the land used for domestic housing.

Although the site of the Manor House and its grounds have been built over, the lodge that used to be occupied by the gardener Mr Dorrell, that marked the entrance to the estate, has survived. Sadly, the grand gates at the beginning of the long, curving drive from Manor Road to the house have gone.

Thomas King Yalland, depicted in 1898, inherited the Manor House and the bulk of his father's fortune in 1897. Apart from his business as a contractor and stone merchant, he interested himself in local affairs and was a talented artist and musician, exhibiting paintings at the West of England Academy and was for forty years voluntary organist and choir-master of Fishponds parish church.

Upper Fishponds House was built alongside the Turnpike Road at Fishponds around 1770, for a Mr James Bridges who was from a wealthy Keynsham family. As an attorney at law, he was appointed clerk to the commissioners when the Enclosure Act of 1781 for 'dividing and enclosing that part of the common or waste land, called Kingswood which lies in the parish of Stapleton', was enacted.

A Cornish Quaker, Joel Leal, set up a school at Upper Fishponds House in 1816. One of his distinguished pupils was William Forster the Liberal statesman responsible for the Education Act of 1870. This woodcut is of the greatest interest being the only known picture of one of the ponds from which the district is named.

Alfred Robinson, a partner in the ES&A Robinson paper and printing company, purchased Upper Fishponds House in 1861 and re-named it Beechwood. He died there in 1901 and his widow lived on at the house until her death, aged 100, in 1934. The house and its eighteen-acre estate was sold in 1934 for £11,400 and demolished in favour of shops and houses.

With the ruins of Beechwood House behind him in 1935, this young man stands on what was to become Beechwood Road. Looking down toward Fishponds Road, note the spire of St Mary's church and the Unionist Club building next to the park.

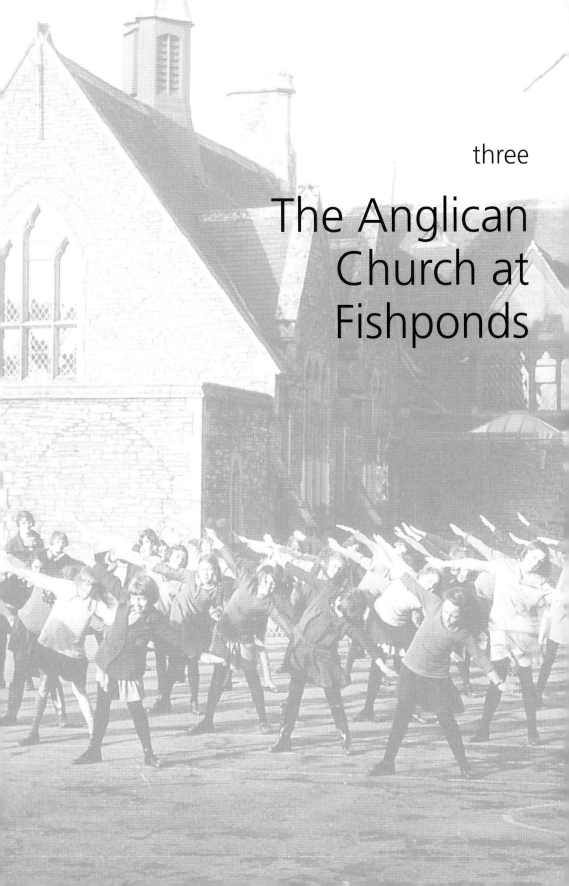

three

The Anglican
Church at
Fishponds

The Anglican Church came comparatively late to Fishponds, being situated within the borders of the ancient Royal Forest of Kingswood. Fishponds was ecclesiastically part of the vast and ancient parish of Stapleton until 1869. Holy Trinity, Stapleton's parish church, first purchased land at Fishponds in 1906 for use as a burial ground but, as the population of the area increased, the need for a place of worship at Fishponds became evident. So the Vestry at Stapleton decided to build a Chapel of Ease on the land they already owned at Fishponds. Trinity Chapel, as the church was first called, was built in 1820, consecrated and dedicated to St Mary on the 31 August 1821 by Bishop Grey.

The Revd William Squire Mirehouse, previously Rector of Closterworth, Linconshire and chaplain to HRH Princess Sophia, daughter of George III, became Perpetual Curate of Trinity Chapel. He was also a magistrate and was Chairman of the Clifton Poor Law Union for twenty-two years. Then, in November 1869, her majesty Queen Victoria and her Privy Council granted Fishponds its own District Chapelry and decreed that the river Frome should mark the division between the parishes of Stapleton and Fishponds. So it was that Trinity Chapel became the parish church of Fishponds to be known as St Mary the Virgin.

An association with the Church came in 1853 when the Diocesan Training College of St Matthias was founded at Fishponds to provide women teachers for the church schools. The original buildings were designed by John Norton, and the later wing of 1904 by Sir George Oatley, famous for Bristol University's Wills building. As the population of the district continued to grow St mary's parish was subdivided to provide two more churches, All Saints, Grove Road, and St Johns, Lodge Causeway.

St Mary's church was built in 1820 as a Chapel of Ease for Holy Trinity, Stapleton. It was first known as Trinity Chapel and seated 700 worshippers with a gallery at the west end. The chapel was consecrated and dedicated to St Mary on St Aidan's Day, 31 August 1821.

The oldest part of St Mary's is the churchyard. An acre of land was purchased by the Stapleton Vestry, for £170 in 1806, for use as a burial ground. During his long ministry (1923-49) Canon John Plumpton Wilson took a great interest in beautifying the churchyard and some of the trees and shrubs he brought back from his travels are still flourishing.

Sunday school children from St Mary's church proudly march with their banners held high past Fishponds Park, accompanied by their Sunday school teachers and the Salvation Army band. The shops in the background were still trading around 1935 and can be seen here, from left to right: No. 769, Samuel Monks, baker; No. 771, Thomas Smith, draper and No. 773, Ralph Bellamy, fruiterer.

Scouts of the 55th Bristol, (St Mary's) Scout Group march along Downend Road on their way to St Mary's vicarage. Note the Number 84, 1930s-type omnibus with its 'Centre' destination board, waiting at the kerbside for the procession to pass.

A Procession of Witness, as the St Mary's Scouts, Cubs and Sunday school march up the Straights, *c.* 1938. Back in May 1909 eleven boys were enrolled into the Fishponds Group of the Incorporated Church Scout Patrols, attached to the Church Lads' Brigade. By 1912 the Boy Scout Association was formed and St Mary's Scouts became the 55th Bristol Troop, led by F.C. 'Skipper' Pearce.

With a spring in their step the St Mary's Sunday school children, Scouts, Cubs and Girl Guides head for St Mary's vicarage in Radley Road, for tea on the lawn, *c.* 1946. The omnibus is one of the Bristol VR series, its number is still 84, but the destination is Hotwells.

The 55th Bristol Cub Scouts assemble on the lawn of St Mary's vicarage, Radley Road, Fishponds, *c.* 1948.

As the population of Fishponds grew, the need for another church within the parish of St Mary's became evident. The first portion of All Saints, at Grove Road, was raised on land provided by Miss Castle of Stapleton and dedicated in May 1906. The enlarged church, seen here soon after completion, was consecrated in 1909 and is a beautiful example of f ourteenth-century, decorated, style.

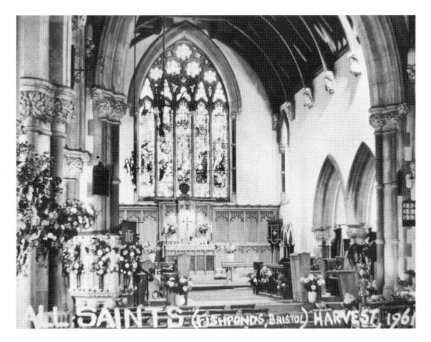

Harvest at All Saints, Fishponds, 1961, showing the altar and east window, the chancel with its marble shafts surmounted by carved caps and the blue Pennant shafts to the Bath stone columns that form a pleasing contrast. All the carving throughout the church is of a very high standard.

The church of St John was also built to serve the needs of Fishponds' expanding population. In 1894 the corrugated iron church with its pitch pine interior, which was already twenty years old, was re-erected on a site, provided by Sir Greville Smythe, in Lodge Causeway. Able to accommodate around 250 people, it was dedicated and opened on 28 July 1894, with the Revd F. Bell as curate in charge.

The first recorded reference of the intention to build a new church was made at a sidesmen's meeting, under the chairmanship of the Revd R.A. Finley in 1904, when a Permanent Church Fund was set up. This picture records the last harvest festival, held in the mission church of St John, 30 September 1910.

The foundation stone of St John's permanent church, Lodge Causeway, was laid on 17 September 1910, by the Misses C. Catherine Robinson and her sister E. Beverly Robinson, daughters of Colonel Robinson, who, when he returned from the West Indies in the 1800s, settled in Frenchay. The new church replaced the iron church seen here in the background.

The workman pause to have their photograph taken while erecting St John's church, Lodge Causeway, 1910. Captain Cotterell-Dormer gave the additional land adjoining the temporary church for the building of a permanent structure. Linden Barker & Son were appointed architects and the builder was Mr W.F. Read of Fishponds, whose estimate of £3,108 was accepted.

The consecration of St John's church took place on Ascension Day, 25 May 1911 and was performed by the Rt Revd George Forest Browne, Bishop of Bristol. The large congregation included Archdeacon Tetley, Canons Alford, Everingham and Weight and twenty other priests, including the Revd C.P. Wilson, vicar of St Mary's, who had supervised the affairs of the mission since his appointment in 1907.

Above: The temporary church of St Bede's, Cherry Tree Crescent, Hillfields Park, was built in 1926 of timber, clad with asbestos sheets inside and out. By 1928 the priest in charge was the Revd George Dymock who, it was said, was a follower of Sir Oswald Mosley's British Union of Fascists. He was certainly an excellent priest, who ran a children's summer club in his garden, a soup kitchen for the poor and unemployed and a rummage shop.

Left: The marriage of Mr and Mrs Saunders took place at St Bede's church, 1959. The church, seen behind the happy couple, closed in 1962 and all that remains is the fine vicarage that was purchased (along with the site) by Brunel Care, who erected sheltered housing for the elderly there. The accommodation opened in 1977.

The Bristol and Gloucester Diocesan Training College at Fishponds, opened in 1853. Its purpose was to train young women to be school mistresses, principally to teach in the National (Church of England) schools in the dioceses of Gloucester, Bristol and Oxford. The original Victorian Gothic buildings were designed by the celebrated architect John Norton, who was born in Bristol.

Known as the College of St Matthias, the Bristol and Gloucester Diocesan Training College is seen here from College Road, (formerly Poorhouse Lane), *c.* 1920. It was founded by the determination and generosity of the Rt Revd James Henry Monk, Lord Bishop of Gloucester and Bristol. As one of the first church colleges in the country, it allowed poor, but intelligent and ambitious, girls to take up professional training and become independent.

Oldbury Court Road leading to the Oldbury Court estate, from Fishponds, *c.* 1910. The gateway to the Diocesan Training College is seen left, while the fields opposite were laid out for domestic housing in the 1930s.

St Matthias' Junior Recreation Room seen here, *c.* 1900. Little comfort here – note the straight backed wooden chairs – the regime too was spartan, as students were required to do the household chores and religious observance was mandatory.

The principal and staff of St Matthias College, 1916. Before the college chapel was built in 1855, daily prayers were read by the principal at 6.40 a.m. and by the matron in the evenings. Lights out at 10 p.m. meant snuffing out the candles.

The principal, matron, staff and students at St Matthias College, 1917. In 1976 the college became a polytechnic, teaching history, English and town and country planning. Eventually, in 1992, St Matthias Polytechnic became absorbed by the University of the West of England.

Fishponds College Practising Junior Girls' School, was built within the college precincts to provide teaching practice for the St Matthias students. Physical training and netball in the playground were all part of the curriculum for these girls in 1936.

As Christmas approached it was customary for the girls of Fishponds College School to provide an 'entertainment' for parents and guests, usually on a classical theme. On the 2 and 3 December 1927 *The Taming of the Shrew* was enacted, with Shakespearean songs sung by the school choir between the scenes. Here the actors and actresses pose in costume.

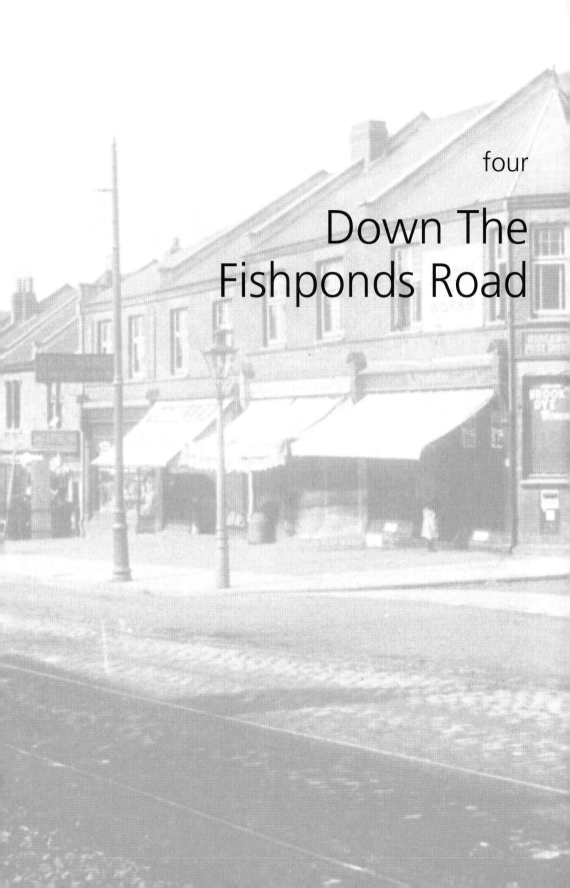

four

Down The
Fishponds Road

The main road through Fishponds has been known by various names throughout the ages. During the seventeenth century it was called the Westerley and Sodbury Way. After the inauguration of the Bristol Turnpike Act, in 1726, it was referred to as the Turnpike Road and by the end of the nineteenth century, as The Ridgeway, before eventually becoming Fishponds Road.

As Fishponds grew, in order to cater for the increased demand for shops, many fronts of Victorian houses, particularly those on the main Fishponds Road, were 'pierced', or had shops built in their front gardens. Two separate ranks of these type of premises still function and bear their original names of Broadway and Cheapside. The shopping facilities along the main road were, and still are, most varied. Along one mile of the road, from the Cross Hands to the Queens Head public houses, 190 different services and commodities can be engaged or purchased and smaller conurbations of shops radiate out from the main thoroughfare. Many of the shops were owned by local families of long standing, like those of Hall (shoes and electrical) and Creeds (butchers), while the names of Orchard and Roberts still maintain a presence on the road to this day.

The Straights, Fishponds
Looking down

This portion of Fishponds Road from the Cross Hands Inn to Fishponds Park is known by the curious name of the Straights, probably because, when travelling from Bristol in the old days, the high road was narrow, winding, muddy and full of pot holes and as the traveller climbed the rise to the inn, the way was indeed 'straight'.

The Cross Hands Inn and Tavern was built on a plot of land, measuring ten perches, which was sold by Zephaniah Fry to James Bridges, of Upper Fishponds House, for £4. A house on the site was sold for £150 in May 1796, but by 1860 it was known as the Cross Hands, seen here, c. 1895.

With the old building demolished in 1904 the new Cross Hands Hotel (that stands in the fork between Downend Road and Staple Hill Road) is situated looking back towards Bristol. Georges Brewery took the lease from Bristol United Breweries in 1956 and by 1962 the hotel was in the hands of Courage, Barclay and Simmonds, who later became Courage's.

Looking up the Straights towards the Cross Hands Hotel, 1907, the shops behind the early motor car are still there. The trees beyond Oldbury Court Road border the Carnival Field, land that remained in the hands of the Vassall family of Oldbury Court until 1934, when the road was widened and shops added. Note the tram lines in the road. At least the boys will be able to hear the tram coming!.

A similar view as the previous one. Here the milkman, with his horse and trap, is delivering milk to the houses. The housewives, or their servants, would come out with a jug for the milkman to fill from his churn.

The carnival field at the Straights was the venue for many fairs and cattle shows around the turn of the twentieth century. Here we have local children taking part in a carnival in 1913, performing their ribbon dance.

These local ladies at the Fishponds carnival of 1913 are probably raising money on behalf of their church and for good causes. They invited visitors to have their fortunes told at the gipsy tent – who knows what secrets were revealed!

What the attraction was that brought so many of the local children together opposite Fishponds Park, in this photograph from around 1910, we shall never know but at least it must have been a happy occasion, judging from their laughing faces.

Looking across Fishponds Road to the park and Manor Road, *c.* 1905. The gas lamp in the road has now vanished and there is a remarkable lack of traffic. The houses opposite Fishponds Park in Manor Road, Nos 1–9, were erected in 1887 and called Victoria Buildings, to mark Queen Victoria's Golden Jubilee year.

It is said Mr John Yalland (of the Manor House) gave the site of Fishponds Park to the old Stapleton Parish Council. There is no record of that land ever being built upon and it is shown on some estate maps as Fishponds village green. However, there is no doubt that Yalland had the park gardens set out in 1888, as is recorded on the drinking fountain at the park entrance.

To mark the coronation of King George V, these Fishponds school children were presented with chocolates in commemorative tins. Perhaps those youngsters under school age did not qualify, the two younger children, centre front, look rather crestfallen.

The philanthropist and authoress Hannah More was born 2 February 1745 at the Fishponds Free School, where her father was the schoolmaster. Hannah and her sisters ran a successful academy for young ladies at No. 45 Park Street. Her engagement to William Turner, of Belmont House, Somerset, was called off by him. Anxious to make compensation for his conduct, he settled an annuity on her that gave her independence.

Hannah More's birthplace still stands near St Mary's church. She published her first play in 1773 and moved to London where her brilliance brought her fame and the friendship of Dr Johnson, Oliver Goldsmith, Sir Joshua Reynolds and the actor David Garrick and his wife.

As the years passed, Hannah developed strong Christian views. Around 1785 she moved to Cowslip Green, near Wrington, Somerset, where, encouraged by William Wilberforce, she and her younger sister (in spite of opposition from both landlords and ordinary folk) opened Sunday schools in Cheddar and district to teach the poor to read. She also wrote hundreds of high-moral toned religious tracts.

Hannah More survived her four sisters and lies buried with them at Wrington church. She left Barley Wood, her second Somerset home, to live her last days at No. 4 Windsor Terrace, Clifton, where she died, in September 1833, aged eighty-eight. Hannah left a fortune of £30,000, the vast majority of which was distributed among charities, religious societies and her schools.

The War Memorial in Fishponds Park was erected on 26 March 1921. The figure was modelled by Messrs Humphrys and Oakes in their studio at Lawrence Hill and four cast-bronze panels contain the names of the fallen connected with the parish. The ceremony was conducted by the Lord Mayor, Mr G.B. Britton MP, Mr Harry Vassall and Col Burges, the original commanding officer of 'Bristol's Own'.

For those who experienced it, the winter of 1947 brings back memories of roads and pavements under a thick blanket of ice and snow, transport difficulties, food shortages, rationing, which was still with us, and electricity cuts. Here, opposite the Vandyke cinema, Bristol City Council workmen clear the last of the compacted ice and snow from Fishponds Road.

The tram terminus was erected in the middle of New Station Road, at its junction with Fishponds Road in 1897. It was a rest house for the drivers of the electric trams at the end of the line from Old Market to Fishponds. Later that year the line was extended to Staple Hill and the rest house was used by the points boys who changed the points to enable the trams to pass up and down the road.

The wisdom of allowing the Bristol Tramways and Carriage Co. to build their drivers' rest house in the middle of the road would certainly be questioned today! However, in 1897, with most commodities being moved and delivered by horse and cart, the terminus did not present a problem, though it did prove to be an attraction to the local children and prospective tram passengers.

The Full Moon Hotel, seen to the left in this picture from around 1910, is known to have been in existence since at least 1781 when the Enclosure Act commissioners posted notices there. In 1910, Stuckeys Banking Co. was using the premises facing the main road, next door to the Fruit and Sweet Supply shop. Mrs Lilian Skuse's stationery and newsagent business became a circulating library in 1917 and ten years later was in the hands of Mr Milton.

Fishponds post office is seen here at No. 755 Fishponds Road, *c.* 1910. The property had been left to Thomas King Yalland on his father's death, in 1897. The newsagent shop at No. 759, next to the Unionist Club, was kept by Mr Quinlan, the only black man in Fishponds at that time.

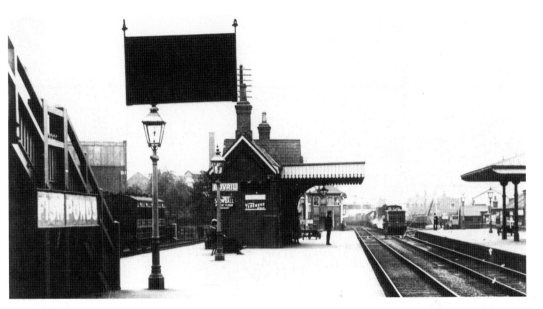

The railway line was first built and opened in 1835 for horse-drawn wagons to haul coal from the pits at Coalpit Heath to feed Bristol's industries. By 1845, having undergone several name changes, the Bristol & Gloucestershire Railway turned to steam engines to provide their motive power. The station originally opened as Stapleton Halt, the name was changed to Fishponds in July 1867 and is seen here in 1920 with a silhouette of the sign indicating platform numbers hanging from the bridge over the line.

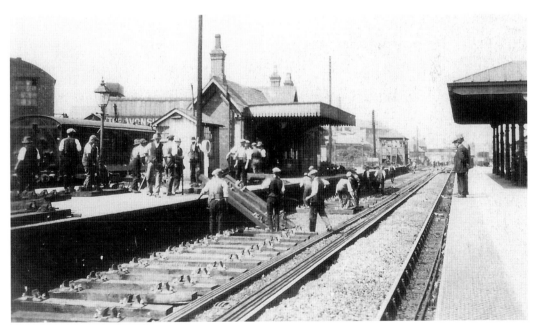

Re-laying the railway track through Fishponds, *c.* 1930. The short shunting line (seen here to the left of the main platform) was also used by the Avonside Locomotive Works to transfer their newly built engines to the main line.

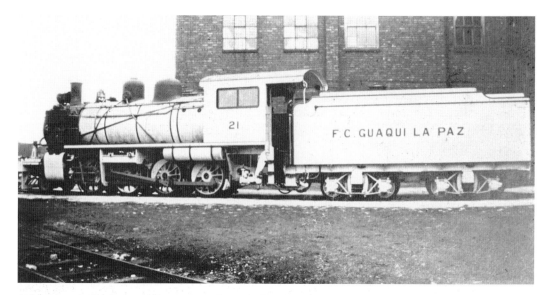

Avonside Locomotive Works was founded in St Phillip's, in 1837, by Henry Stothert & Co., who then became Stothert, Slaughter & Co., in 1841. Edwin Walker joined the company in an effort to extricate them from financial difficulties but was unsuccessful. A new company was formed using the old Avonside name and moved to Filwood Road, Fishponds, in 1905. Their locomotives, of various gauges, were exported all over the world.

The Avonside Engine Company's football team are seen here during the 1916/17 season. During the trade depression of the 1930s, Avonside went into voluntary liquidation in November 1934. The goodwill, drawings and patterns etc., were purchased by the Hunslet Engine Co., in 1935, when the plant and buildings were sold off.

Approaching Fishponds railway station from Bristol, on the Midland Railway line, this steam train is passing under the footbridge that spanned the line from Hockey's Lane to Justice Road.

The Midland Railway took over the Bristol to Birmingham line in May 1845. The station at Fishponds opened in April 1866 and after operating for almost a hundred years, finally closed on 7 March 1966, a victim of Dr Beeching's cuts. The station buildings were demolished, the line lifted and the former trackbed was converted into a cycle path-cum-walkway.

Originally the Masons Arms (dating from 1839) this public house was renamed the Railway Inn, upon the arrival of the railway nearby, in 1866. It then became the Railway Hotel in 1891. When the pub came into the hands of Halls Brewery in 1976, it was called the Peckett Flyer but in due course the name was changed again to the more familiar Railway Tavern.

In the nineteenth century it was common for some commercial enterprises to give small change in the form of tokens that could only be used as currency at that establishment. This practice was carried on by William Milsom when he was landlord of the Railway Inn sometime between 1866 and 1891.

Trinity Wesleyan Methodist church, No. 800 Fishponds Road, was opened on 28 February 1894, at a cost of £3,700 and designed by the architect William Paul. The general architecture was Decorated Gothic (fourteenth century-style); the front was constructed of blue Pennant stone, with dressings of Corsham Down and red Mansfield stones and polished Aberdeen granite columns on the nave window and entrance.

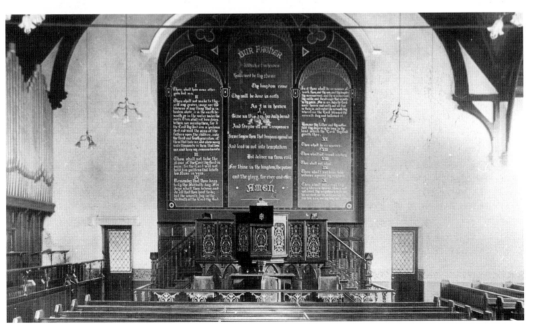

Internally, Trinity church was about 60 ft by 41 ft with two transepts and had seating for 450 people; all the fittings of chapel and school were made of polished pitch pine. The schoolroom, behind the church, was 45 ft by 38 ft with four entrances and was surrounded by classrooms of various sizes separated by glazed screens, which were easily removed.

Unfortunately, by 1965 Trinity Methodist church had developed building faults that were too expensive to rectify and the congregation combined with Ebenezer Methodist church, Fishponds Road, and decided to build a new church in Guinea Lane. Trinity was subsequently demolished and replaced by a Tesco supermarket. The building is currently occupied by Poundstretcher.

Looking towards Bristol, this row of houses was originally known as Nos 1-5 Broadway, Fishponds Road. Mr Alfred Holman, a watchmaker, had started business in Argyle Road in 1918 and moved into No. 5, next to the Methodist church in 1927, when all five houses had shop premises built into their front rooms downstairs and the garden walls were demolished to provide a forecourt. Today, the business is conducted by Miles Boyd, Mr Holman's grandson.

A modern Broadway seen here around 1980 with Flooks Wine shop at No. 1; Catherine & Jon, hairdressers at No. 2; Stuckey & Sons, outfitters at No. 3; Wesley English's, hardware at No. 4 and Holman's, jewellers at No. 5.

This very substantial Pennant-stone building was erected in 1903 at No. 697 Fishponds Road (next door to the police station) to house a branch of Lloyds Bank Ltd, with Fredrick G. Tucker as manager. Today the front garden walls and the railings have gone but Lloyds still occupy the building.

Bethel Gospel Hall, Chapel Lane (pictured here in 1974), was used by Christians of various denominations throughout its existence. Built in 1833 as a Baptist Meeting House, it temporarily housed the Wesley Reformers (1850) and was purchased by the Primitive Methodists for £325 (1859) before their move to Wharf Road. It also housed the Salvation Army from 1899-1916, then the Pentecostal Christians from 1928. In September 1969, after 136 years of religious use, Beacon Motors used the chapel as a storeroom and it was finally demolished in 2003 to make way for a food store.

The Primitive Methodist's new church was Zion; No. 644 Fishponds Road at its junction with Wharf Road, seen here in 1972. Built of local stone, with freestone facings, it cost around £1,500 and opened on 28 March 1875, when a procession, formed at the old chapel of Bethel, marched along Fishponds Road to their new premises. Damaged by German bombers on 16 March 1941, when three houses were destroyed and eight people killed, it was then used commercially until it was demolished in 1996. The Bristol Import Centre now uses the site for car sales.

Mark Whitwell, the philanthropist and social reformer, laid the memorial stone of Zion Primitive church in September 1874. The chapel, seen here celebrating a Sunday school anniversary on Whit Sunday 1917, could seat 500 people on low open pews of varnished pine. At the south end was a platform, in the centre of which was a reading desk, and below, a lesser platform containing the communion table all railed around with neat ornamental ironwork.

Fishponds police station, pictured here around 1907, was opened in 1870 and cost about £2,900 including the sum of £12 set aside for the fitting of Moules Patent Earth Closets. By 1877 a horse-drawn fire engine was kept at the rear of the station where there were also some stables. It became redundant around 1970, after lying abandoned for some years. Redland Housing Association and Bristol City Corporation turned the building into older peoples' dwellings, which opened in 1982.

This panoramic sequence of three pictures looking towards Fishponds Road were taken from North Devon Road in 1935. The first shows St Mary's Parish Hall (or Hannah More Memorial Hall), built in 1912, with a large room, which could accommodate 200 people, a billiard room, lounge, committee rooms, and so on. The lower portion was used for Sunday school purposes. Re-named Wayland Court, it currently provides accommodation for people suffering from mental illness.

This second picture shows a view through Hinton Road to the Vandyck cinema across open land that is now covered by Lambrook Road and housing. To the right in the picture is the rear of Trinity Methodist church and its large Sunday school building.

The third picture of the sequence again shows the rear of Trinity church, which is next to the back of the row of shops known as the Broadway, then the back of Lloyds Bank. Next door is Fishponds Police Station identified by its tall chimney. The open land in the foreground now accommodates the bungalows built in Lambrook Road, with the brook still running left to right at the bottom of their gardens.

The Vandyck cinema, 1960, was designed by W.H. Watkins to seat 1,200 people and opened on 5 November 1926. The last film to be shown here on Saturday 28 July 1973 was Ringo Starr and David Essex in, *That'll be the Day*. Kirk Douglas featured in *A Gunfight*. It became a Mecca bingo hall, the doors of which closed in 1996. Later the Wetherspoon chain reopened the old cinema as a pub called the Van Dyck Forum in 1998.

This photograph, taken in 1926, is advertising a film that is 'showing tonight at the Vandyck' called *The Last Frontier*. The 'Indian' sitting in the back of the car was Mr Brain, the cinema pianist in the days of silent films, while the second 'Indian' was the cinema doorman whose duty it was to keep the kids in order. The cinema manager and owner-driver of the car, with its spare petrol cans on the foot board, sits behind the windshield that proclaims: The indians have arrived.

On Christmas Eve, 1828, William Parker leased a plot of land from Charles Henry, Duke of Beaufort, to build a house. Parker soon turned his home into a beerhouse and by 1859 his heir, Robert, purchased the Portcullis Inn from the Duke for £240. Robert Parker's descendants sold the inn, together with an adjoining cottage, to Georges Bristol Brewery for £5,000, in 1878. The Portcullis, pictured here in this rare photograph from around 1900, passed into the hands of Courage Barclay Ltd, for £12,600, in 1967.

In the first half of the nineteenth century it was the voluntary organizations, namely the British and National Societies, which pioneered education for the masses – state assistance was negligible. Dr Bell's National School was built in 1850 at a cost of £1,346. The inclusion of Dr Bell in the name indicated that the school would adopt the Bell system whereby the master would run the school with the help of Pupil Teachers and Monitors.

Dr Bell's schoolroom is seen here in 1950. After assembly and morning prayers, glass doors were slid across to divide the hall into separate classrooms. Under the Hadow Scheme in 1934, when Mr E. Cooke became headmaster, Dr Bell's became the Junior Boys' School. In 1945 the school title was again changed to Dr Bell's Primary Boys' School to conform with the Education Act of 1944.

Class 7 at Dr Bell's Junior Boys' School, 1937 pose for the camera with their teacher, Mr Weber, left and headmaster, Mr Edwin Cooke, right.

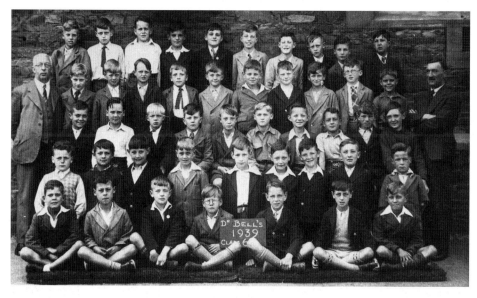

With the Second World War imminent, Class 8 at Dr Bell's Junior Boys' School are pictured here in the summer of 1939. In the back row, from left to right are: Leslie Arthur; 'Lulu' Bryant; Michael Bricknell; Peter Bull; Brian Dicks; Geoffrey Wheeler; Donald Groves; –?–; –?– and ? Boulton. Second row, from left to right: Norman Horton; Derek Baker; –?–; –?–; Peter Brown; Gordon Lovell; Derek Knox; Vernon Patch; Keith Beese and John Butler. Third row, from left to right: Michael Hamblin; Dave Nicholson; John Nash; Pete Moncrieff; –?–; Dennis Gould; Billy Green; Fred Wheeler; Norris Lamb and ? Maggs. Fourth row, from left to right: Keith Jefferies; Bernard Davies; Reg Leonard; Ray Sturgess; 'Donkey' Davies and Brian Pepler; Ronald Pow; John Heap, Douglas Maguire. Front row, from left to right: Jack Payne; Dennis Milsom; Johnnie Worth; Leslie Helps; Gordon Perry; Kenneth Miles and Douglas Crane. The headmaster, Mr Cooke is on the left and teacher, Mr Sage, is on the right.

Dr Bell's Church of England School was demolished in 1965 and the plaque that was originally mounted on its front wall declaring: Dr Bell's National School, was set in a section of garden wall, where it could be seen from the main road. By 2001 that wall had become unsafe and a danger to the school children, so it was taken down. The plaque was removed to a safe place with the intention of re-erecting it within the current building.

The modern Dr Bell's, seen here in 1970, is set well back from the main road. It was combined with St Matthias College School to become Dr Bell's College Church of England (voluntary aided) Junior School. In the year 2000, with the closure of St Matthias College Infants, Manor Road, and the building of a new infant school at the Dr Bell's site, it now operates under the name of St Matthias and Dr Bell's Church of England Voluntary Aided Primary School.

A British (Nonconformist) School was erected in Hockey's Lane in 1853, where the schoolmaster, Mr Jacobs, taught a mixed school of 225 pupils, with one assistant and four pupil teachers. The building was also used by the Wesleyan Reformers, who later became United Free Methodists. By 1879 the school was in decline and the building in the hands of the Methodists. It became a furniture store in 1965 and by 1995 was a sports injury clinic.

The United Free Methodists moved from Hockey's Lane to their new church they called Ebenezer, on Fishponds Road, in 1881. Known locally as the Clock chapel, for obvious reasons, the congregation retained the old school/chapel in Hockey's Lane for use as a Sunday school. After some eighty-three years the church closed and became yet another motor car tyre and exhaust centre and is currently a car sales outlet.

Built in 1879, probably as a dwelling house, by 1900 a Miss Weeks was the beer retailer at the Stag's Head off-licence, No. 682 Fishponds Road, near Hockey's Lane. In 1915 the licence passed to Alfred Thomas Hutton until 1944, when the Stag's Head came into the hands of Miss Elsie Smith who retained the property until she sold it to Mr Morris for the development of his MWM Motors garage in 1965.

This view from the rear of the Stag's Head off-licence was taken just before the demolition of the premises. The shadowy roof in the distance is that of the former Methodist school in Hockey's Lane, which still stands today and features a plaque set into the front of the building inscribed: 1853 Free Methodist School.

The building next door to the Farrier's Arms, seen here in 1973, was formerly the blacksmith's workshop. Both are thought to have been erected around 1760. It was first mentioned in the directories in 1868 as being occupied by 'George Alsop Daws, Smith and Beer House Keeper' but the beerhouse had no name! In the passage of time it simply became known as, The Farriers. Today the public house stands alone. The smithy, that later became a garage, was demolished for road widening.

From 1894 to 1915 Palmer Bros, biscuit and cake manufacturers, were in business at No. 617 Fishponds Road (that property is now within the City Glass Complex). By 1916 Palmer Bros had moved across the main road into the redundant Ebenezer Wesleyan Chapel at No. 700 Fishponds Road. The biscuit factory, pictured here in 1979, was enlarged over the years and the new buildings completely enveloped the old Ebenezer Chapel.

This aerial view of Hockey's Lane, from around 1970, was commissioned by John Anderson of Fishponds Plant Hire, who, with his brother Dave (of Mercia Metals), operated from the premises left of centre. To the left in this view, is Palmer's biscuit factory and to the right is the former railway goods shed standing alone in its yard and beyond that can be seen the trackbed of the Midland Railway before its conversion to a cycle path.

In 1991, in order to build the Safeway supermarket at Fishponds and its attendant car park, a huge site had been cleared that reached from the main road alongside the Farriers Arms back to the old railway line. All the commercial premises on the east side of Hockey's Lane were demolished. This evocative picture, looking west, shows the shell of Palmer's biscuit factory with the silhouette of the original Ebenezer Wesleyan Methodist Chapel, founded in 1831.

Regent Place is pictured here just before the First World War, all the buildings are still standing on Fishponds Road. The land was owned by Gloucestershire magistrate Charles Castle, who lived in Stapleton village, when local butcher Isaac Ford was using the site in 1861. The summer of 1864 saw the clearance of the site and the construction of the present buildings. No. 6 Regent Place was first known as the 'Black Horse' and was to become one of the tied houses of the Red Cliff Brewery, Bristol. It was William Hobbs who changed the name of the public house to the Golden Lion in 1877.

Grandfather Hall married Hester Purdy and kept the boot and shoe shop at Regent Place. He is seen here, at the rear of his shop, with his son Albert.

Emily and Miriam Hall, who in their turn carried on the family tradition and kept the boot and shoe shop at Regent Place. The shop was sold when one of the sisters died.

This tiny chapel built just off the Fishponds Road at Alexandra Park (formerly Monks Lane), seen here in 1975, is shown on the Stapleton Tithe Map of 1839 as a: Meeting House, Landowner, Hester Smith. By the 1980s all that was left of the meeting house was a small two-storey building, by then in use as a garage and store at the rear of Dixon's Wallpaper Shop, No. 643 Fishponds Road. The building was cleared away when the premises of Randall's Timber Merchants was redeveloped in 1996, in favour of Riva (now Gala) Bingo.

Mr Daniel Bawn, grocer and fly (a one-horse hackney carriage) proprietor seen here with his family outside his shop, No. 774 Fishponds Road, corner of New Station Road, c. 1897. The shop also housed Fishponds' first telephone sub-exchange and would have had a 'call room' for the use of the public – not that the operator would have been very busy, for the 1894 list of subscribers shows only five non-commercial telephones in Fishponds.

Alexandra Park Junior Mixed and Infants' School was built by the Bristol School Board and opened in 1901. Then, in 1934, it was promoted to a senior school. A victim of educational reorganization, the school became the East Bristol Adult Education Centre from 1988.

The staff at Alexandra Park Junior and Infants' School seen here in 1923. Back row; from left to right: -?-; -?-; -?-; Miss Mitchell; Miss Hunter; -?- and Miss Smith. Front row; from left to right: -?-; Miss Stevens; Miss O'Hara; Miss Grant and Miss Swingler.

The staff at Alexandra Park are seen here nine years later, in 1932, the year the headmistress Miss Cathleen O'Hara married Joseph Bishop and held an evening celebratory supper party at the Berkeley Café, Bristol, with a string quartet, vocal trios and a short cinema programme by Mr H.Salanson. Back row; from left to right: -?-; -?-; Miss Jennings and Miss Mitchell. Second row; from left to right: Miss Monks;-?-; Headmistress Miss O'Hara; -?- and -?-. Front row, from left to right: Miss Norris and Miss Smith.

Alexandra Park School infants, Class 1 from around 1928, shows lots of smiling faces but Miss Mitchell needs to reassure one reluctant pupil.

Alexandra Park infants in their classroom, *c.* 1930. All the children are well behaved and neat and tidy, note the pictures and drawings with samples of handwriting on the wall behind the young scholars.

The children at Alexandra Park Junior School pause around the May pole, 1932, during a dancing practice to celebrate the coming of spring, which they will perform for a May Day celebration.

The Cross Hands, No. 627 Fishponds Road, was one of the many beerhouses in the district to come into existence following the introduction of the 1830 Beer Act, whereby anyone of good character could buy an excise licence for two guineas and sell beer direct from their house. The Cross Keys is seen here sporting its 1891 frontage of red and yellow brick.

Fishponds Baptist church began when fifteen members of the Foster Baptist church at Downend broke away to hold a meeting in the chapel of Dr George Gwinnett Bompas's house (Fishponds Private Lunatic Asylum), on 7 May 1841. The church at No. 15 Downend Road, Fishponds, was founded in 1847 and opened in 1851 with Dr Bompas the driving force behind the project. He did not live to see the work completed.

Members of the Sea Ranger Ship, SRS *Bristol*, met at The Den over stables in Hockey's Lane and are seen here at the Baptist church, Fishponds on 29 July 1945. Back row; from left to right: Nancy Poolman; Kathleen Lumber; Joyce Edwards; Marie Elms; Carmen Fleming and Nora Scull. Middle row, from left to right: Olive Young; Jean Hicks; J. Norton; J. Coles; V. Hepburn; Vera Chapman; Nellie Dumble; M Dowse; Betty Stone; Jean Highmore and Joyce Hall. Front row, from left to right: Denise Edgar; Valerie Butler; Julie Brand; Joyce Monks; Sylvia Pocock; Lorna Every and Margaret Bryant. The leader, not portrayed, was Miss Winifred Trowbridge, a teacher at Staple Hill School.

This tiny cottage at No. 621 Fishponds Road, thought by some to have originally been built as a toll house, was situated next door to Billy Hill's greengrocers and was pulled down in the mid-1980s and replaced with Forget Me Not, a florist.

With factories being built in the first decade of the twentieth century, at the lower end of Lodge Causeway it became necessary to widen the bridge that spanned the railway line. Here, in 1926, the work is proceeding, watched by a single male figure (right) and two boys hanging over the parapet of the bridge. The houses and wooden railings (left) have long disappeared.

A Victorian house, which was in private occupation until 1902 when a Mary Carpenter home was set up there 'for the protection and training of feeble-minded girls', was situated at Nos 598-600 Fishponds Road, at the junction with Lodge Causeway. Beset with financial problems, the home closed in 1919 when the cost of keeping a girl rose to 12s 6d a week. From 1924-30 part of the house was used by the Order of the Druids Society and within living memory became a registry for births and deaths. It then became Newton's Car Sales and Garage, but was demolished around 1978.

Next door to the Elmgrove post office and stationer, kept by Edith Biddlecombe, on Fishponds road in 1921, were: Stokes the Chemist; Magnus Roderson, shop keeper; Thomas Wren, hairdresser; then Eastman's, butcher; Victoria Steam Laundry; George Oliver, Draper; Horace Horton, greengrocer and Martin's, ironmonger. The tram is just passing Grove Road opposite Lodge Causeway.

George Orchard's ironmongery shop, at No. 589 Fishponds Road, can be seen in this picture from 1925. Noted for their range of ironmongery and household furnishings, George and his sons also operated an extensive paraffin oil delivery service. The advertisements in the shop window exclaim: Fresh Cats Graves 4d 1lb; Puritan Soap 41lbs 2/- and Our Cash Mangle Prices Cannot be Beaten.

The Orchards are one of the long-established business families in Fishponds and in 1944 Orchard's furniture shop, on the corner of Ernestville Road, needed a replacement window. Next door, at No. 594, was George Humphry's newsagent, while Jasper Hatcher kept the Digby outdoor licence at No. 590. Today, John Orchard continues the family tradition with his pet supplies store on the site next door to his father's former ironmongers shop.

This block of five, spacious Victorian houses at Stoke View, built from the local Pennant stone with Bath stone dressings, and their front garden walls topped with iron railings, are typical of the larger residences built along the Fishponds Road from around 1880.

This view, from around 1975, of those same houses gives a good idea of how, when the population of the area increased in the first two decades of the twentieth century, so did the need for more shops. In many instances, the shops were not custom-built but simply erected in the front gardens of the houses along the main road.

Travelling up the hill towards the main shopping area in 1911, the horse-drawn carts keep clear of the tram lines. The first shops past Eastville Park were: Watson Rust's, newsagent; Charles Mitchell, watchmaker who shared premises with hairdresser George Lowe; then Brown's, greengrocer, and Joe Dickman, fruiterer.

Built by Charles King, around 1860, the Star beerhouse (pictured here in 1974) was named after the Star Pit, one of the Duke of Beaufort's coal mines that was formerly situated on the opposite side of the road, at the top of Star Lane. Founded in 1883, the Black Arabs Football Club, which later became Bristol Rovers, used the Star Inn as their headquarters during their 1894/95 season, playing all their home matches at the Rudgway Ground, which lay between the Fishponds Road and Ridgeway Road.

Doris Williams (above left) was born in Star
Cottages (later No. 543 Fishponds Road) (right)
next door to the Star Inn in 1899. She married
Arthur Leopold Chapman (above right) in 1923.
As the years passed they were blessed with three
children; Vera, John and Margaret. The cottage was
small, with a front garden that reached down to the
main road. Vera was four when this picture of her
with two-year-old brother John on his tricycle was
taken in 1931. By 1956 the cottages were falling
into disrepair and were subsequently demolished
and replaced by a garage owned by the Harris
Motor Co.

The well-known Alcove Lido (as seen in this rare photograph) at Fishponds was originally a clay pit owned by the Fishponds and Bedminster Brick & Tile Co., situated on a ten-acre site, south of Fishponds Road, to the rear of No. 466. The extraction of the clay for brick-making commenced around 1880 and was considerable. The clay was loaded onto drams and transferred to the works for processing.

The company excavated the clay at Fishponds until they went down deep enough to hit the local water table level, uncovering a vigorous spring in the process. As it proved impossible to get rid of the water in sufficient quantities, so the pit started to fill and the work had to be abandoned. The company went into liquidation in 1908, while still retaining ownership of the land.

Access to the clayworks site, brickworks and kilns was situated at nearby Ridgeway Road (formerly Crooked Lane), where the works offices were alongside No. 20, (subsequently renumbered No. 39) seen here, *c.* 1900. The works foreman, Levi Gunning, lived next door. Currently the office building, still recognisable, has been converted into a dwelling.

The flooded clay pit was used by an angling club in 1913, then purchased by local builder, Mr H.E. Green, who built a pavilion, changing rooms, diving boards, sunbathing terraces, and so on, and opened the Alcove Lido in May 1934 – it became a great success. By the 1970s the popularity of the lido waned and the old pit was filled in and by 1980 its new owner sold the site to Barrett Homes who built Marina Gardens, a series of flats and maisonettes, on the reclaimed land. Today, the floating pub/restaurant has gone and all that remains of the lido is a pond used by an angling club.

Ridgeway post office, at No. 369 Fishponds Road and the corner of Huyton Road, *c.* 1920. Note the wooden blocks between the tram lines in the roadway. In spite of a change of name to Upper Eastville sub-post office, the premises that incorporated Cavill's grocery shop continued as such until at least 1973.

Dating from the fourteenth century, Ridgeway House, seen here in 1936, was the only true manor house, in Fishponds. Formerly standing at the head of Red Hill Drive, its domains reached down to the river Frome. Purchased by Richard Berkeley in 1568, the house was used as a lunatic asylum by Dr Nehemiah Duck in 1920. The Revd Henry Malpass had a school there from 1865-70, which was attended by W.G. Grace. It became a YMCA hostel before being converted into flats in 1931 and demolished, *c.* 1938.

When seventy acres of land for Eastville Park was purchased by the Bristol City Council from Sir J. Greville Smyth, for £30,000 in 1888, there was an outcry in the local newspapers against the transaction, as the land was outside the city boundaries. However, in 1897 when those boundaries were extended to take in Fishponds, the wisdom of the purchase became obvious. The large ornamental lake was constructed in 1909, providing work for unemployed men. This view, from around 1913, shows the church of Holy Trinity, Stapleton, in the background.

The Queen's Head, opposite Eastville Park, has certainly been in existence since 1839, for it appears on the Stapleton Tithe map as a beerhouse, occupied by John Smith. Seen here in 1921, with the addition of a Victorian frontage, when two charabancs full of men (probably members of the Royal Antediluvian Order of the Buffalos) are about to set off on an outing. As the coaches are fitted with solid rubber tyres it can only be hoped their journey was not too arduous.

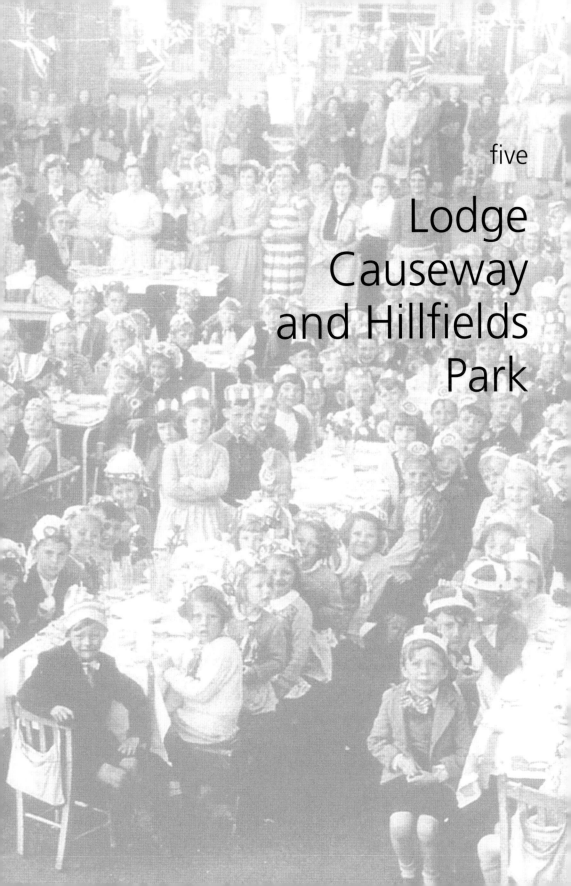

five

Lodge
Causeway
and Hillfields
Park

On 1 November 1897, Bristol extended its boundaries to take in both Stapleton and Fishponds. At this time two of the staple industries in the area, coal mining and stone quarrying, were in decline but the situation was saved for the local workforce when several well-known industrial companies (having outgrown their premises in the City of Bristol) moved to Fishponds and built new factories adjacent to the main roads and the railway. When the electric trams were extended to Fishponds and Staple Hill, in 1897, this also meant that people could travel to and from Fishponds for work.

The Provincial Land Co. sold and let plots of land bordering the causeway for housing and soon Mayfield Park and Chester Park were developed. Cock Green and the Crooked Lane enclosures, with its pastures and arable land, were of particular interest to the industrialists; both were situated at the lower end of Lodge Causeway. Cock Green was favoured by Pountney's Pottery and Crooked Lane is better known today as Ridgeway Road.

The First World War intensified the industrial activity in the Fishponds area. The new factories were put on a wartime footing: Palmer's biscuit factory – making army biscuits – and Brazil Straker's engineering works – turning out army lorries, shells and aero engines. After the war, Fishponds' expansion from a village into a thriving suburb of Bristol was almost complete.

In 1919 the Bristol Corporation purchased 128 acres of land for £18,322 and, under the National Housing Scheme, commenced building its first housing estate. The first houses were erected at Beechen Drive in the district known as Hillfields Park. It was David Lloyd George who had coined the phrase 'Homes fit for Heroes' and it would have been possible for a disabled ex-serviceman to live and sleep in the ground floor parlour of one type of house, said to have been designed for that purpose. In due course the estate was extended when a further 51 acres was acquired.

In the early days of the Hillfields Park estate, as some of the older, long-established residents were at pains to point out, they were not from slum clearance areas. In order to qualify for a council house they had to be employed and earn enough to afford the rent of about 15s a week. At first, lighting and cooking was by gas (electricity was not connected until 1931/32) at a halfpenny per unit. Council rules were strict. The interior house walls could only be distempered and the privet hedges, that enclosed the generous gardens, had to be kept trimmed. As the estate developed, so did the shopping and medical facilities at Lodge Causeway. In later years, many of the tenants took the opportunity to exercise their right to purchase and many of the former local authority houses are now in private ownership.

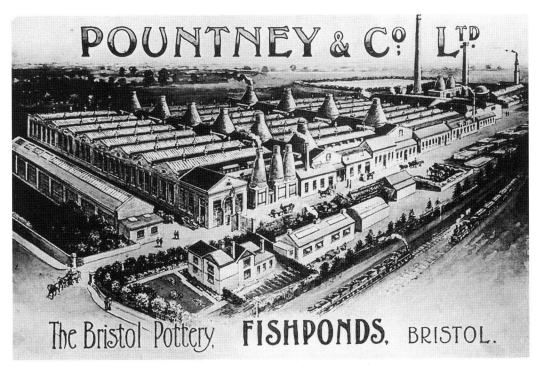

POUNTNEY & Cº LTD

The Bristol Pottery, FISHPONDS, BRISTOL.

Above: Pountney's Bristol pottery moved from St Phillip's Marsh to the lower end of Lodge Causeway in 1906, where an entirely new factory was designed with the most modern techniques then available. Washbasins, lavatories and white, glazed tiles were made alongside tableware and specially toughened pottery intended for institutional use. They all needed to be fired in the kilns.

Right: This picture from the *Bristol Evening Post*, February 1954, shows foreman 'Ernie' Dagger entering a biscuit oven balancing a sagger full of pots on his head. The first, or biscuit, firing fixes the clay into its permanent shape, the article can then be decorated or glazed before being returned to the kiln for a second firing.

Even when the old kilns were outdated and replaced by modern gas and electric-fired tunnel kilns, Pountney's still retained two of the old beehive kilns to give the pottery a traditional look. Around 700 people were employed at the pottery in its heyday, about half of whom were women and almost all lived locally.

In 1962 Pountney's purchased the goodwill, moulds and pattern books of the Royal Cauldon Pottery, who had gone into liquidation. Sadly the large Fishponds' factory became uneconomic and it was decided to relocate to Camborne, Cornwall, under the name of Cauldon Bristol Potteries Ltd. This proved to be a poor decision and by 1971 Cauldon Bristol was purchased by A.G. Richardson & Co. Ltd. Meanwhile, the old Pountney site at Lodge Causeway was sold off for £235,000.

Chester Park Church of England School, first opened in 1884 in two houses in Chester Park Road and became a board school in 1894 when it lost its affiliation, though not connection, with the Church. By 1896 the children moved to their new schools that were erected in Lodge Causeway; where the infants' class started as a separate department with Miss Ferris as headteacher. The infants' school is shown here with the junior school in the background.

On 18 June 1897 the children were given a week's holiday for Diamond Jubilee Week, to mark sixty years of Queen Victoria's reign, and from 1 November that same year, the administration of Chester Park School was transferred to the Bristol School Board. Here, fifty children from the infants' school, wearing pinafores to protect their dresses, pose for the camera with their teacher in 1914.

Fortunately, Chester Park School suffered little damage during the Second World War, when some sixty-six children had been evacuated from the school to the Taunton area. The 150 or so that remained at the school spent many daytime hours in the air-raid shelters that had been constructed in the playground. When the hostilities came to an end the school held a great VE Day party in the playground.

Father Christmas arriving in the hall at Chester Park School, 1956. Watching with the children are headmistress, Miss Cox, her staff and the Revd Bennell from St John's church, next door.

Brazil, Straker & Co., founded at St Philip's in 1893, opened a new engineering factory at Lodge Causeway in 1907. The company manufactured omnibus engines and chassis that were driven to London to have the bodies fitted. By 1909, 70 per cent of London's buses were supplied through the company's London sales outlet. A young man called Roy Fedden joined the company soon after its relocation. He came with a design for a new car that was a great success. As chief engineer, Fedden went on to design, build and race cars at Brooklands.

During the First World War, the factory produced staff cars and lorries, as well as munitions and the first aero engines to be designed and built in the Bristol area. Soon after Roy Fedden (seen here front row, centre) had designed the famous Jupiter aero engine in 1918, the company was bought out by Cosmos Engineering Co. and the engineering side of Brazil Straker's was sold off, as Cosmos was only interested in aero engines.

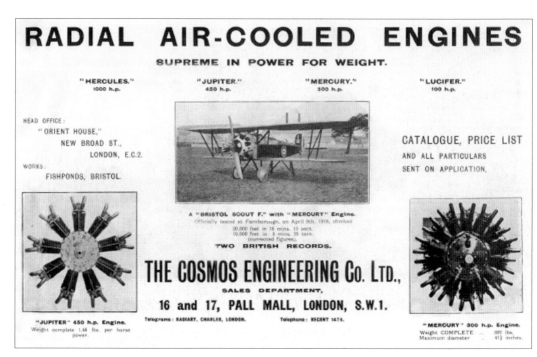

Comos had overstepped themselves and went into liquidation in 1919. Roy Fedden and his team were bought out by the British and Colonial Co. at Filton (the forerunner of the Bristol Aeroplane Company), where the engine department was founded in 1920. Roy Fedden went on to become Sir Roy and was probably one of the greatest intuitive engineers in history.

Founded in 1820 by William Parnall, who traded as a weights and measures manufacturer in Wine Street, Bristol, Parnall & Sons Ltd diversified into shopfitting and during the First World War became involved with the manufacture of aeroplanes in various premises around Bristol. When Cosmos Engineering went out of business, Parnall & Sons Ltd acquired their former factory premises at Lodge Causeway in 1923, with a view to further expansion.

Even when Parnall's main factories were situated in Bristol, they had maintained a foundry at Parnall Road, off Lodge Causeway, hence the date plaque of 1911 on the façade of a house in the road. The occasion for this picture of Parnall's shopfitters foundry, from around 1900, is unknown. The foundry was later used by George Adlam & Sons Ltd, iron founders and brewers engineers.

One of Parnall's extensive workshops at Fishponds in 1924. When the old-fashioned straight shop fronts were superseded by island windows and arcades in bronze metal, one famous contract executed by Parnall's in 1929 was the fitting of bronze shopfronts and display cases at the underground station of Piccadilly Circus, London.

Although the backbone of Parnall's shopfitting company was woodworking and joinery workshops, seen here in 1924, the company also became active in the field of refrigerated display and storage cabinets. Expertise gained in the fabrication of plastics led to the formation of a plastics division for point of sale display and packaging material.

Examples of Parnall's work could be found in a bewildering variety of places: shops, prestige stores and banks. They also made internal fittings for passenger liners, like the *Britannic Tourist* dining room, (above) and installed many public rooms aboard the *QE II*, including the first-class cocktail bar, library and a staircase through eight decks.

In 1931 Tansad was added to the Parnall operation, manufacturing a quality range of executive, management and clerical desks, storage units, and so on and, as illustrated in 1934, office chairs. Then in 1979, Parnall's & Sons were bought out by G.E.C. who in turn sold the company to C.H. Holdings, a London conglomerate, who after the works had suffered a couple of disastrous fires, went into receivership in May 1991. The site is now used as a car supermarket.

In the late 1800s when the Mayfield and Chester Park areas developed just off Lodge Causeway, Walter Bracey's greengrocer's and grocer's shop, at what became No. 44 Berkeley Road (seen here in 1900), served the local populace.

Elisha Smith Robinson was the founder of a famous paper and printing company of Bristol. He moved his business from Baldwin Street to larger premises at No. 2 Redcliffe Street in 1846 and two years later he was joined by his younger brother Alfred and the company became ES&A Robinson Ltd. In 1922 the company built a cardboard box factory at Filwood Road, seen here, *c.* 1930.

Robinson's manufactured waxed paper for the provision of hygienic food wrappers in 1924. A subsidiary company, the Robinson's Waxed Paper Co. Ltd, moved to a new factory at Fishponds in 1929. The factory was enlarged several times and this picture shows the new frontage of 1958. Robinson's merged in 1966 to become the Dickson Robinson Group and went out of business in 1996. The buildings are now in the hands of Zanetti & Bailey, marble floor specialists.

Mr Weber came from Switzerland and opened his chocolate factory, seen here around 1975, at Lodge Causeway in 1914. A noted radio enthusiast, before the inauguration of the BBC in 1922, he obtained an amateur transmitting licence and broadcast musical programmes that could be picked up locally on the early, homemade crystal sets. Mr Weber's factory ceased production in 1964.

St Joseph's Roman Catholic church, Lodge Causeway and corner of Forest Road, seen here in 1980, was opened in 1925, at a cost of £10,000. The architect was Sir Frank Wills and the builder Mr Clark of Fishponds. The new church replaced a corrugated iron mission church on the site, that had previously been used by the Redemptorists Fathers at Park Lane, Kingswood, Bristol, until 1911.

This view of Lodge Causeway, taken around 1930, shows the clock tower of Cossham Hospital, surrounded by trees in the distance. The car to the left is parked outside Carey's hardware shop, next door to Madame Lilian Rawnsley's hat and millinery business at No. 265 and Fredrick Tully's tailor and outfitting shop at No. 267. While opposite, on the forecourt of the Berkeley Arms, 'outdoor beer' licencee, Annie Walker, watches the photographer.

Looking down Lodge Causeway towards Fishponds Road, around 1956, the shops on the right include Cadle & Sons, Bollom's the cleaners, a hairdresser and Bridie Free's wool shop. Also in view on the right, just in front of the Morris Oxford car, is a once-familiar sight, a Brooke Bond tea van; its driver making a delivery.

Built as an 'outdoor beer licence' shop in 1879 (with a house attached and further accommodation above) Chester House, at No. 312 Lodge Causeway and the junction of Chester Park, was a substantial building when Gerald Harris was the beer retailer here in 1935, the date of this picture. He was followed by Gerald Towse in 1944 and his wife Ethel after him. Chester House became a branch of Lloyds Bank in 1962 and to date has remained as such.

When building commenced on the Hillfields Park Housing Estate, a plaque was erected on the façade of a pair of houses in Beechen Drive declaring: 'These houses were the first to be erected in Bristol under the National Housing Scheme in the year 1919. E.W. Savory, chairman of housing and town planning committee'.

When ES&A Robinson built their cardboard box and wax paper manufactories at Filwood Road, Fishponds, in order to encourage their employees to move to a new part of the city, they arranged for houses to be built to accommodate them at Maple Avenue, Hillfields. The houses could be purchased from the company by payments stopped from the workers' wage packets. As the Bristol Corporation owned the land, ground rents were paid directly to them.

As the Hillfields Estate grew, so did the need for schools and Hillfields Park Infant School opened in 1927, soon followed by the junior school in 1929. This aerial view shows the infant school fronting The Greenway and the new junior school that was built 1931, in an arc behind. Hillfields Avenue crosses diagonally at the top right corner, with Market Square beyond.

Opposite below: Miss A.L. Mitchell was born on 18 November 1901 and, like her two sisters, she qualified as a school teacher. She never married but devoted her life to teaching children, first at Alexandra Park, Fishponds, later at Hillfields Park, where she is seen here with her infants' class and finally at Redcliff Infants' School, Bristol. She died on 30 January 1987. Her epitaph should read: To teach is to touch a life foreverever.

Hillfields Park Junior Mixed School, B.S.A.A. Junior Championship, 1938. Back row, from left to right: Mr Mogford, headmaster, R. Henderson; E. Jacobs; Mr J.J. Baulch, sports master. Front row seated, from left to right: F. Smith; A. Milton; R. Dewfall. The young man seated centre, holding the cup is Arthur Milton, who completed his education at Cotham Grammar School, Bristol. Excelling at ball games, he joined Arsenal Football Club in 1945, playing in the 1952/53 season when they were champions of the football league. He signed for Bristol City 1955. Arthur also played cricket for Gloucestershire from 1948. He played 620 first-class games, six times for England and on his test debut scored 104 not out against New Zealand in 1958.

Other local titles published by Tempus

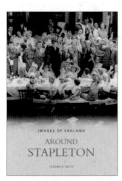

Stapleton

VERONICA SMITH

Illustrated with over 200 photographs, this pictorial history is a remarkable evocation of life in and around the Stapleton of yesteryear. From timeless vistas of the Frome Valley to snapshots of the bandstand at Eastville Park, local sporting heroes at Alexandra Park, Fishponds Lido and Coronation Day parties, this volume provides a nostalgic insight into the life and changing landscape of the area around Stapleton.
07524 3059 9

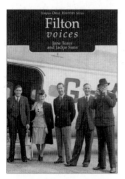

Filton Voices

JANE TOZER & JACKIE SMITH

This book brings together the personal memories of people who lived and worked in Filton from the 1930s, vividly recalling the farms and fields before they were lost to housing. The voices tell of childhood games, the close-knit community, shops and entertainment, as well as the devastating effects of bombing raids on the aircraft factory. The stories are complemented by a hundred photographs drawn from the private collections of the contributors.
07524 3097 1

Haunted Bristol

SUE LE'QUEUX

This selection of newspaper reports and first-hand accounts recalls strange and spooky happenings in Bristol's ancient streets, churches, theatres and public houses. From paranormal manifestations at The Bristol Old Vic to the ghostly activity of a grey monk who is said to haunt Bristol's twelfth-century Cathedral, this spine-tingling collection of supernatural tales is sure to appeal to anyone interested in Bristol's haunted heritage.
07524 3300 8

Bristol Times revisited

DAVID HARRISON

This book is a collection of some of the articles drawn from the first year of the Bristol Times supplement of the Bristol Evening Post. Each extract recalls an aspect of the city's lively, and sometimes turbulent, history. From tales of fairs, workhouses, riots and gaols, to accounts of star appearances at the Hippodrome and the success of Fry's chocolate factory, each piece provides an insight into Bristol's past.
07524 2844 6

If you are interested in purchasing other books published by Tempus, or in case you have difficulty finding any Tempus books in your local bookshop, you can also place orders directly through our website

www.tempus-publishing.com